Japanese Maple

Acknowledgements:

"Conifer", "I Was Stupid When I was Young", "Iris", and "Silver Queen" were previously featured in the Spring 2016 issue of the *Good News Paper*.

"Grown Up Problems" and "Stomach Acid" were previously featured in the Fall 2016 issue of *Fluent Magazine*.

Thank you to the editors of these publications. Special thanks to Ed Zahniser for the shove.

For my family, and for the mountains.

I.
Japanese Maple

My dead grandmother holding me in that one photograph
I never knew her – but I knew you
At least once – in that basement on your birthday
Just another atom in my sight

Stomach Acid

The way the river smelled at seventeen
Aluminum distractions and sleeping in cars
An accidental smokescreen deflecting
The inevitable ache of time

Appropriate nostalgia for a soft second
Precluding the balancing act between
Mountains and bars, streams and girls,
Hay fields and cheap drugs

Reunion therapy bourbon and stomach acid
Xanax counselor to quiet the kids
It was I who killed the sun, and spit in the face of the summer
When I moved to the city and tried to hide my accent

Bottle Rocket

You can't burn too bright if you've always been faded
Like the bad tattoos you got in college
From the artsy kid who worked weekends at the coffee shop
I heard his mom got sick and he moved back home

It's just a wrinkle in your dress shirt
A slight crack in your brow
Some days my eyes are more green than blue
I named your freckles while you slept

Peaceful beginnings wash into tired nights
Choking on air thick with sulfur and lighter fluid
Stand back – I'm a professional
Count the stars, my little bottle rocket

River Lot

Every pleasant memory waterlogged
By that simple, numbing blue
The largemouth dodge my recreational attempts
Disrupting their necessary kill – nature's order

That beach was no stranger to escape artists
Infamous deceit executed with legendary cowardice
At least, that's how I will remember you
Not the gentle words or leather-soaked tobacco teeth

I'll never forgive the world for letting the bad guys get away
But I can certainly try to forget
Lofty dreams of my offspring swimming
Their eager casts ignored by bass

Three Choices

The branches we'd shake, one eye closed
To simulate a false sense of balance
Just a couple of pups punch-drunk
On banquet beers and Marlboros

My shining knight, brotherly rival, truest heart
There was a different awakening in you
Ashamed and afraid you locked it in shadow
But bottled poison will rot the jar

And now you've crossed oceans I cannot pronounce
Tasted fruits I cannot digest, sang songs I cannot hear
I still treasure our boredom, which sparked a sweetness
Defined by sneaking alcohol through windows

Grown Up Problems

I never met an autumn I didn't want to bury
Beneath cracked oak and compost
Complete with empty liquor bottle headstone
To accompany the useless undergraduate eulogy

A serotonin stream just inches out of reach
Left with fractured chords and nightmares
Painted in ex-lover hues: blotted strawberry blonde,
Cerulean stroke, a shade of olive

We offered our howls to the solstice sky
They were greeted with silence and the problems of grown ups
Ancient dust from a neglected campfire mirroring
A piece of heaven not suitable for wolves

Paper Cuts

The years greeted you fork-tongued and sacred
And if you'd known it would be this severe
You might have considered taking that extra dose
During Christmas break junior year when she was gambling again

Chasing roman candle lights on the screen
Milking one biological act of creation
For an eternity of wrecking balls aimed
Directly at the one thing you've loved – your protector

A deceptive sermon found in the bottom of Sunday's ashtray
Just visualize your freedom and you will be absolved
Of every paper cut in your lungs
That you measured between the tar and the fang

Boy Name

She used to meet me every morning by the lake
Palm cool upon my fevered flesh
My anxious eyes always locked on the escape
Daydreams diluted by cattails and sun perch

Awake and aware I am hostage to this shell
I naively bend strings to force pretty sounds
Paint over the portraits to make a shape familiar
As the comfort you'd kill to remember

And now she chases me through dark hallways
Begging for help every night
I feel my insides boil and burst
While I ignore her as she's eaten alive

Japanese Maple

It took me years to grasp the notion
That you cannot translate the wind
Into anything remotely audible
Like a sea of locusts kissing off the drought

Perfect songs of faith and anger – crooned to the mountains
Echoed in the hollows, sustained in the ash
The longing is palpable – the ache is true
I miss everything all the time

The county line was just a stain
On her vulnerable, nameless daughter
Whose penance would be served the same spring
That the Japanese Maple wilted before it could drink up the sun

II.
Clay & Dust

Please remember this:
I will love you forever

Even if you broke my bones
I can set them
Even if you drained my blood
I can replace it
Even if I let my shadows grow too long
I can catch them

You didn't deserve any of it, either
I forget if this is for you or me

Silver Queen

There was a moment when I could still
Discern my name breathed through
The silver queen fields –
Syllables choked on chlorophyll
Consonants drunk on dandelion
But the clocks were desperate for calibration
So I forgot about time

I had friends who never settled
Or complained about rough beginnings
Refused to accept anything but the sun
Trophies held with blistered fingers
Mountains built on third-degree degrees
But they expected reciprocal dialogue
So I forgot about people

And once I owned a mirror
That only entreated honesty
Historical like the kind that used to exist
Countenance reflected like obsidian
Background blurred with motor oil
But it swore I saw the truth
So I forgot about me

Moorefield, WV (Everybody Hates Everything, Everywhere)

I want to cherish this moment
the same way I wanted her in the summer of '99
swimming pools and barbecues –
char-grilled adolescence

It's all fine until you wake up old and broken
I don't remember why I wanted to be with you
but goddamn - tri-county fair, grandma's old Buick,
tape deck, homemade wine – I was fucking alive

The sun bronzed your face like apache war paint
"I love you to the moon," she said
but tonight -
it's just a waning thumbnail

I Was Stupid When I Was Young

Sunshine was a luxury that we couldn't afford back then
In fact, I don't recall a single window in the entire house
Saturday nights spilled over into Sunday's shame
I remember quieting my keys as I'd sneak to my room
Head still dizzy from the previous night's poison
But I cannot blame the chemicals
It was my hand that wrote the prescription
My mouth that invited the lightning
My brain that begged for the heat

On more than one occasion I probably almost died
It's easy to confuse exhaustion with giving up
I remember wanting nothing else but to just feel normal
Twenty-three years (give or take) of living on polar extremes
Trading one form of therapy for another, only to end up the same
But I cannot blame the method
It was my eyes that read the label
My guts that savored the storm
My lungs that inhaled the venom

I got out the way most do – a gas pedal and a scholarship
But I didn't completely dodge the shadows
They still hold a piece of me ransom on the weekends and the long nights
Because you can't stare into the darkness for that long
Without letting your curiosity test the waters
But I cannot blame the absence of light
It was my grief that closed the blinds
My soul that sought the shade
And my heart that let you go

Conifer

How do we measure the cost of sacrifice?
Is it magnified by the essence of youth
Or the ease of frailty?
When does one accept that we are nothing but moving ghost bones?

I used to fancy myself a conifer
That I would remain – defiant, evergreen
While I watched those around me splinter
And crumble into the soil

But I suppose I was more like corn silk
A temporary protector of something golden
A bone saw handle delivering the means
To amputate what had rotted and been absolved of use
A wild dog muzzle holding back the severity
Of our actions, and the reality of our dreams

The desire to control is unnatural and violent
So I made myself deciduous so I could die after each frost
And try to feel nurtured long after
I've lost my milk teeth

Hutton Run

Washed away in the same breath
That speaks easier after four drinks
That's the way it happens these days
Instead of 6 a.m.
Bathroom floor-anxiety-psychosis
Calling every distant family member
That maybe won't be ashamed
To hear your fractured voice at this hour

I'll be damned if I don't remember
Being young, and brown from the sun
That is more generous to my cousin
(but I don't call him that, because we are brothers)
But his mother has an indian name
So god has made him darker than I
And as children we would follow the creek
That cuts through our grandfather's farm
Mapping every bend, and drawing
Every unique creature that we'd encounter
And each night recount these adventures
Out loud before we pass into rest
In the same room that our fathers shared as boys
But my sickness had started, and when the dawn
Greeted my sleepless eyes I had already
Held full conversations with my brother
While he was sound and still

A million years and sore muscles later
My father discovers a satellite
That tells him our creek has a name
A normal man-given name
But I don't acknowledge this
Because men have no right to claim
Something so primitive and pure
So I close my eyes and recall
My sleep-talking brother
Speaking rapidly of salamanders
And from across the room I know
That he is smiling with eyes shut

Nicknames For Grandparents

Winter came in with a frost that was deafening
Pure, innocent silence
But somebody must answer for this
A single accident that defines a lifetime

Of scabbed knees, fishing poles, and homecoming dances
Nicknames for grandparents, and schoolgirl crushes
November's temperature was permanent for you
Forever frozen in pieces of Polaroid and Kodak

They say we carry her in our heart, but they really mean the mind
Which is a fallible instrument
Susceptible to abuse and deception beyond belief
Unlike the heart, which simply hardens
Not unlike the ground does in these sober months
When any semblance of hope is drained from a parent's eyes
Because what are children other than hope?
A vanity of lineage? A side effect of pleasure?
No. I believe that word is sufficient.
So carry it at your convenience
And send it up towards heaven
The way the snow kills the youth

I Can't Sleep Anymore

"Congratulations," you said as you floated down the stairs
Like a drunk paper airplane – I thought you were beautiful then
And not some cosmetic illusion, a golden slice of sun
Defiantly choking out the clouds

"I'm so proud of you," whispered (or slurred) through enough
Valium and Irish Rose to drown any professional south side lush
And in these formative years you've now mastered
The back-alley waltz that's been romanticized on bathroom stalls,
Bar napkins, & sweaty palms shaking at last call

"You were always my angel," a dangerous olive branch for the vulnerable
- my brain is a retired dancer, and my heart a smoking pistol
Born on the wrong side of the tracks – blame geography,
Or the circumstance of class, you know in your deepest isolation
That this is not your fight

"It's just a friend at the door," and I knew what you were doing then
But a blind eye helps you sleep at night when ignorance keeps the peace
I wish we could trade all of those cold mornings of withdrawal
For the boredom of health, but there is no compromise of sweetness
When you practice the hospitality of a spider

Iris

My vision failed me in my twenties
Faded into neon and a lightless apartment
Propelled by the slow rot of compulsion
Saturated by years of empty decadence

A moon spell plea to restore my faith in clay and dust
But the stars colluded against me in a jealous coup
Left me shattered with lead shoes and a blood thirst
To rival a starved shark in the deep end

Somewhere along the way, our lineage was preserved
By flight at the hands of torture and repetition
There is nothing noble in avoidable slaughter
Listen: there has never been a better time to run

Pay no mind if the mountains mock you
They simply wish they had your speed
Dream of all that nameless water that you would never see
Focus your iris and draw your own maps

www.ingramcontent.com/pod-product-compliance
Lightning Source LLC
Chambersburg PA
CBHW070756050426
42449CB00010B/2497